GARAGE SALE SUPERSTAR

How to Make the Most Money Possible at your Garage Sale, Yard Sale, Rummage Sale, Estate Sale, or Tag Sale

[Almost Free Money Series, Book 2]

By Eric Michael

Copyright, Legal Notice and Disclaimer:

This publication is protected under the US Copyright Act of 1976 and all other applicable international, federal, state and local laws, and all rights are reserved, including resale rights: you are not allowed to give or sell this Guide to anyone else.

Please note that much of this publication is based on personal experience and anecdotal evidence. Although the author and publisher have made every reasonable attempt to achieve complete accuracy of the content in this document, they assume no responsibility for errors or omissions. Also, you should use this information as you see fit, and at your own risk. Your particular situation may not be exactly suited to the examples illustrated here; in fact, it's likely that they won't be the same, and you should adjust your use of the information and recommendations accordingly.

Any trademarks, service marks, product names or named features are assumed to be the property of their respective owners, and are used only for reference. There is no implied endorsement if we use one of these terms. Finally, use your head. Nothing in this Guide is intended to replace common sense, legal, medical or other professional advice, and is meant to inform and entertain the reader.

Copyright © 2012 Eric Michael. All rights reserved worldwide

Garage Sale Superstar

ISBN: 978-1484193563

CONTENTS

- INTRODUCTION 5
- GENERAL INFORMATION 8
- GARAGE SALE AND YARD SALE TIPS 9
- GARAGE SALE ORGANIZATION 11
- GARAGE SALE ADVERTISING 15
- GARAGE SALE DAYS OF THE WEEK 18
- GARAGE SALE START TIME AND HOURS 20
- WHEN TO START YOUR GARAGE SALE 21
- GARAGE SALE SIGNS AND STICKERS 23
- SIGN SIZE AND DESIGN 24
- SIGN CONSTRUCTION 26
- GARAGE SALE STICKERS 28
- GARAGE SALE PRICING 30
- GARAGE SALE PRICING GUIDE 32
  - Media Items 33
  - Clothes 33
  - Household Items 34
  - Collectibles 35
  - Video Games & Systems 35
  - Toys and Games 36
  - Holiday / Christmas 37
  - Outdoors 37
- AFTER YOUR GARAGE SALE: GETTING RID OF YOUR STUFF FOR FREE 39
- YARD SALE TIPS 41
- CONCLUSION 43
- WEBSITES AND LINKS 44

INTRODUCTION

Welcome to the fun and exciting world of Almost Free Money. This is the second book in our successful series of e-books written to assist people in making more money at garage sales, yard sales, and second-hand stores.

In the first book in the series 'Almost Free Money', I discussed different avenues for making money on items that are available in most areas for free, or under $1. I discussed locating items at second-hand locations, such as garage sales, yard sales, thrift stores and flea markets, as well as places where you can find materials to sell for free while you recreate. I also gave readers detailed instruction on how to sell such items online, or at physical locations like garage sales and scrap metal sealers.

In this, the second book in the Almost Free Money series, we will discuss making "almost free" money by selling your property at free venues like garage sales, yard sales, estate sales, and tag sales. As a veteran of visiting over 1,000 garage sales in the last ten years, I can provide specific examples of what works for garage sale hosts, and what does not. I also have a background as a garage sale investor. I have been buying items at garage sales, and flipping them on eBay and Amazon for over twelve years. I can tell you what "flippers" are looking for, and how that can benefit you. You will earn how to advertise to all garage sale shoppers including flippers. We will discuss how to make the most money at your next garage sale by efficiently advertising and promoting your garage sale, so that hundreds of people will be lining up at your garage sale. You will learn how to effectively price your garage sale items, so that you get the most money possible without giving your customers sticker-shock.

I will also talk about the best way to organize your garage sale and lay out your displays and tables, so that you sell the most items and make the most money, while clearing out some of the clutter from your home. We will go over the best days to hold your garage sale or yard sale, and how long your sale should be open to maximize profit.

Garage Sale Superstar is leveraged with the background knowledge of the owners of Garage Sale Academy.com, a diverse website dedicated to assisting garage sale hosts in managing their garage sales and increasing profits.

I will also review several excellent sources to advance your knowledge base with further reading on the internet and there are several affordable opportunities to further your research and take the next step toward making your annual garage sale into a new business venture.

GENERAL INFORMATION

There are many areas that can affect the bottom line of your garage sale:

1. The Starting Time and Ending Time of your Sale
2. The Days of the Week that you are Open
3. The Time of Year for your Sale
4. The Organization of your Sale and Tables
5. Advertisement of your Sale
6. **Garage Sale Signs**
7. The Location of your Yard Sale
8. The Content of your Items
9. **Garage Sale Pricing**
10. Dealing with Customers

We will discuss all of these important aspects of your garage sale in detail in the following chapters.

GARAGE SALE AND YARD SALE TIPS

Let's start with some garage sales tips that will help you to make the most money from your potential garage sales items:

- Before you even start looking for stuff to sell, contact your neighbors, friends and relatives and decide on a weekend at least one month in the future that will work the best for everyone. Not everybody needs to be a cashier / host at the sale, but they will at least need to have their items priced and at the sale location. Multi-family garage sales will attract more shoppers and make you more money every time. The larger your sale is, the more customers you will get, and the more stuff you will sell. We will discuss multi-family garage sales more in-depth later.
- Holding your garage sale weeks in the future is great for several reasons. It allows you time to go through all your storage areas to find items to sell. Go through your attic, crawl space, garage, closets, and sheds to find stuff to sell. Go through the boxes that nobody has been into in years. You may have garage sale gold in those boxes! Also check all of your dresser drawers for clothes that are not worn anymore or kids' clothes that don't fit. Clothes make excellent money at garage sales, especially name brand items.
- Make a general list of the large high money items that you intend to sell at your garage sale, and have your co-hosts do the same. Compile one list for the sale that contains all of your big-ticket items so that you can include those items in your classified ads and online advertisements.

- Advertise your garage sale for TWO weeks before your sale, not just the prior week. Be creative with the title of your sale. Come up with a cool theme - 'Manly Garage Sale', 'Moms and Tots Sale', and 'Sportsperson's Yard Sale' are examples. We will cover advertisement along with additional garage sale tips in detail later.
- Check your garage sale inventory for items that will make you more money on eBay or Amazon. If you have never sold on these internet sites, don't be nervous! They both have exceptional instructions for getting started that any 12-year old can follow. You just have to go for it! Media items, collectible items, and designed clothes are areas where you will make significantly more money on the internet than at a garage sale!

GARAGE SALE ORGANIZATION

Organizing a garage sale is a free way to make significantly more money at your garage sale. You would think that every garage sale host would be organizing a garage sale to make the most money, wouldn't you? Common sense should tell you that if your yard sale looks good, and if the best items are closest to the customer's reach, that you would end up making more money. Yet, how many garage sales have you been to where stuff was strewn across tables, clothes are pulled off hangers, stuff is out of sight in boxes, and items are not even priced? I have seen hundreds of yard sales like I just described. Do you know how much stuff I bought at those sales...? Very little.

Here are some tasks that should be done before your garage sale is to be held:

1. Check out the chapters on getting ready for organizing a garage sale, yard sale, tag sale, or estate sale: **Garage Sale Tips**, **Garage Sale Advertising**, and **Garage Sale Signs.**
2. Organizing a garage sale should not be a one-person chore. Assign co-hosts to complete tasks - advertising, making signs, rounding up display materials, checking to see if there are garage sale sign, sale permit, or parking regulations where you live, getting change, and arranging for babysitters. There's plenty to do for everybody!
3. Get all of your garage sale items in one place several days ahead of time. Figure out how much volume you have, how many tables you will need and get everything priced BEFORE THE SALE. If your garage

sale starts with un-priced items, you may not get time to get stickers on them, and most will go unsold.
4. After you get an idea of your volume, figure out what you will need for tables and displays. Find yourself a table and chairs for a check-out table. If possible, set up your tables and clotheslines the day before. Figure out where you will have people park their vehicles. Organizing a garage sale is easier after planning.
5. Get at least $50 in change. You will need at least $20 in one-dollar bills, and $5 in quarters. Decide who will collect money and give that person a money apron or fanny pack, so that the money is NOT sitting on a table in a box.
6. Round up an extension cord or two, (so you can test electric items, and run your fan for comfort, if it is hot). You may also want a supply of batteries for testing battery-powered items. Do not give away your good batteries inside sold items. They are expensive!
7. Call your co-hosts and make sure that everybody is still going to be there for the sale, and who is bringing what. You don't want any surprises the morning of your sale. Make sure that someone brings the coffee and doughnuts, and that somebody has arranged for lunch and cold drinks, if it is hot!

There is also plenty of organization work to do on the morning of your garage sale:

- Get there early! You do not want to be scrambling around at the last second, or even worse, organizing a garage sale after the sale has already started.
- Set up all tables and displays that you could not set up the night before. Make sure that everything is priced. Get everything out of boxes, so customers can see your items. Don't make your customers dig through your gross boxes.

- Have your co-hosts handle some tasks. One person should be handling the money. One person can greet people and answer questions (and perform kid-duty, if required). If you have additional support (sounds like a military recon, doesn't it?) have somebody assigned to organization. This is very important to your sales.

The Organization person should be keeping your sale looking good. Think of your yard sale like a clothing store. Make your shelves and tables look sharp. Keep moving items closer to the customers when stuff gets pushed to the back of the tables. Make sure clothes are spaced on your lines, and not falling off of hangers. Check to see that your items are not getting mixed in with other categories of items. Make sure toys are not on the ground where people can trip on them. Make sure that stacked items are not going to tip over and that your aisles are spaced correctly.

Ten tips for effective organization and spacing of your garage sale and yard sale tables, displays, and traffic flow:

1. Make sure that tables and displays are spaced out far enough that people are not bumping each other, or tripping each other. Make sure there is nothing on the ground that people could trip over or slip on when organizing a garage sale.
2. If at all possible, make your tables line up in straight lines, and make them the same height (waist-high tables for adults work well). Organize you tables so there is an obvious flow. Try to keep people moving in the same direction, as much as possible.
3. Put your large items and expensive items so that people see them when they first get to your sale.
4. Put your pay table at the front of your sale, and have a greeter to say hello to people. Customers will spend more money if they feel comfortable. They will also be more likely to buy stuff from you if they like you.

5. Make sure that your higher priced items are closer to the front of the tables, so people see them first.
6. Make sure people can reach all of your items, even little old ladies and kids. Keep toys where kids can see them and reach them. If you want to sell some toys, make sure kids at your sale can pick them up and play with them.
7. Run a clothesline inside your garage, and hang up tops, jackets, suits, dresses and all name brand clothing. It's OK to keep T-Shirts, shorts, and kids clothes folded up tables.
8. If you run short on tables, you can make tables from sawhorses or stacked boxes with wood paneling on top. Make sure you cover them all with clean sheets or table cloths.
9. When items sell, move unsold items from the backs of the tables to the fronts, where people can see them better. Space items out more, so there are not large gaps. Later, take down tables to make your sale look like it has more stuff.
10. When your garage sale is winding down, lower your prices and start offering deals! You don't want to clean up all that stuff, do you?

GARAGE SALE ADVERTISING

Garage sale advertising can effectively double the traffic to your sale. Free classifieds, Craigslist, and newspaper classifieds are options available to hosts. Speaking from the perspective of a long-time garage sale picker, I will tell you that 90% of the thousands of garage sales and yard sales that I have been to were found either on classified ads or online classified sites.

What does that mean for you, the garage sale host? You can't rely on simply throwing up a couple of rummage sale signs, if you want to get good traffic to your site. Sure, you will get a few shoppers, but you are holding the garage sale to make some money, and organize your home, so make the effort to advertise your garage sale. You can advertise garage sales for free. Here are some general advertising tips to help you get the most out of your advertising, and people to your sale:

1. Take advantage of listing your garage sale in free classified ads for two weeks prior to your sale, not just one week. Many newspaper classifieds are received on Wednesday or Thursday, and the extra week allows those people who don't immediately browse their classifieds to find your yard sale.
2. Garage sale ads should be posted in multiple locations, both online and in newspapers. It does not take very long to make an online classified listing for your garage sale on Craigslist and in your local 'Home Shopper' classified newspaper.
3. Make sure that you list your sale on Craigslist. Most garage sale pickers start planning garage sales routes by finding good sales to visit on Craigslist these days.

4. Garage sale signs are for navigation to your sale, not garage sale advertisement! Make sure your signs are visible from the roadway, so that customers can find their way to your sale. Do not rely on signs to bring in a high volume of traffic.

I will tell you exactly what I look for when using online and newspaper classified ads to select garage sales to visit during garage sale picking routes. In perusing hundreds, maybe thousands of yard sale ads, I am constantly surprised by how poorly worded many ads are that are in the classifieds. It is not rocket science. This is what your garage sale classified ad should contain:

- The particulars. Clearly state the **days of the week and dates** that your sale will be open, the **Times that your sale starts and ends**, and the **address**. That should be the first line. You may wish to add the closest main intersection, but most people either have GPS, or can use MapQuest on their cell phones these days.
- If other families are contributing to your sale, list your sale as a **'Multi-Family Garage Sale'**, or **'Neighborhood' Garage Sale**. It gives the impression that you will have lots of good swag at your sale. The other families do not all have be physically present at your site. If they gave you some stuff to sell, that's good enough for me.
- Descriptions that include phrases like **'years of accumulation'**, **'1st sale in years**!', and 'Grandma's first ever garage sale' would pique my interest. How about yours?
- List some interesting **items that will be for sale** at your garage sale. Garage sale advertising really should not be any different than a sales pitch at a department store. Make people interested in going to your sale. What are people looking for that you can use to

get them to your sale? Collectibles, Sports Cards, Vinyl Records, Good Furniture, Baby and Kids Clothes, Toys, Old Books, Sporting Goods, Hunting and Fishing Gear, and Name-Brand women's clothes are several particulars that will bring in customers. Also list large **high-value items** like newer electronics, bicycles, lawnmowers, outdoor play sets, large collections like stamp collections and music collections.

- Specify whether you allow **'Early-bird Sales'**. You have to understand that even if you started your sale at 5AM, you would still have a couple of die-hards there are 4:30. Early-birds can be good for getting a jump-start on your sales, but often, hosts are still trying to get their sale set up, and dealing with taking money and answering questions from these people can be annoying. I've always thought that it was inconsiderate of the early-birds anyway. I never go to yard sales before the start time, for that reason.

The following is an example of a free garage sale advertisement at a free yard sale classifieds site like Craigslist. I honestly don't see any need to pay for classified ads anymore, with the exposure that you get with Craigslist garage sale ads. Take your money and put it into good yard sale signs and garage sale price stickers instead. Garage sale advertising can be done for free!

"5-Family Neighborhood Garage Sale. 5525 St. Joseph Street in Montcalm. Friday May 4 and Saturday May 5. Sale Open 7AM-3PM. NO EARLY SALES. Large accumulation, 1st sale at this address! Collectibles, Big-screen TV, CD'S & records, Food Processor, fishing gear, duck decoys, lots of man stuff & tools, women's name brand clothes, kids clothes & Toys. Holiday decorations. See you here!"

GARAGE SALE DAYS OF THE WEEK

As veteran garage sale hosts, we can give you good advice on which days you should be open. Should your yard sale be open only on Saturday, or on Friday and Sunday, too? What are the best garage sales days? We have been to hundreds of garage sales, and hosted many more. We can tell you what works, and what is just wasted time.

Saturdays are BY FAR the best garage sale days to be open. On busy weekends, you can make 60-70% of your garage sale money between 8AM and noon on Saturday. So, what does that tell us? #1, you had better be open for business between 8AM and 12 Noon on Saturday. #2, all of the other days only make up less than 30% of your sales, if you consider that you will probably make some additional good sales on Saturday afternoon past the 60-70% prime time period on Saturday morning.

Here are some other things to consider when deciding which garage sale days to be open:

- Saturdays are MUST-DO days for garage sales. You MUST be open early on Saturday mornings, and be open through mid-afternoon on Saturday, at a minimum. Obviously, the longer you are open and the more days you can stay open, the more sales you are going to have.
- Fridays are also good days for garage sales and yard sales. You should at least have you rummage sale open for half of a day, on Friday afternoon.
- You will get some of the really good customers on Friday, including the hard-core pickers and collectors.

If you have many collectible items or expensive items to sell, make sure that you are open on Friday!
- Fridays can also allow you to try selling some of your more expensive items for higher prices. Try putting your max price on these items for a while on Friday. If they don't sell Friday, lower your prices a bit on Saturday morning.
- Sundays are poor days for holding yard sales. Many people go to church on Sunday mornings, and others gather for Sunday brunch or other meals. There is generally very poor traffic on Sundays. There is also a perception that all of the good stuff at garage sales is gone, only leaving picked-through trash.
- You may want to try to hold your garage sale around the first and third weekends of the months, when people often receive their paychecks. People also generally pay bills at the end of the month, so get them at the beginning of the month when they still feel like they can spend money your sale.

GARAGE SALE START TIME AND HOURS

When is the best garage sale start time? When is the best time to start a yard sale?

Even experienced garage sale hosts struggle with these questions. This is probably because there is no absolute right answer for a garage sale start time. If you click on the prior link, you will see some suggestions for maximizing your sales by being open at the right time on Funtime.com.

After holding and shopping hundreds of garage sales, yard sales, rummage sales, and estate sales, I will throw in my two cents on what your garage sale hours should be. I will discuss what time is best to start your garage sale, when to end your garage sale.

WHEN TO START YOUR GARAGE SALE

Your garage sale start time can be affected by several things, including the time of year you hold your sale, and where you live. If you live in hotter climates, you will want to take advantage of the cooler weather in the morning and start earlier. For the same reason, if you hold your sale in August when it is usually sweltering hot, start earlier.

Here are some general guidelines for when to start your sale:

1. Never start your sale after 9AM. Never! Most veteran garage sale pickers start garage sailing at 7AM, and are stopping for brunch by 10AM. Starting your yard sale after 9AM tells customers that you don't care much about your sale. I never go to sales that start after 9.
2. The earlier you can start your sale, the more sales you will get! The early bird gets the worm, and many senior citizen shoppers are up and out of the house by 6AM. Start your sale at 7AM and you WILL get some early sales, plus if you are the first sale open in your area, the majority of the veteran pickers will be at your sale first! This is especially true if you took my advice about garage sale advertising and listed a bunch of enticing items in your classified ad or Craigslist garage sale ad that collectors would be interested in buying from you.
3. Make sure you address EARLY BIRD shoppers. These are the people that show up at your house an hour before your listed garage sale start time. While annoying, these people often buy multiple items from garage sales. You can jump start your sales, and still address these people by putting up a large sign that says "ALL SALES BEFORE 7AM (or your start time)

ARE DOUBLE STICKER PRICE. Make sure you stick to that policy, even ten minutes before your start time.
4. Make sure that you have **prices** on all of your items BEFORE your yard sale starts, preferably the night before, so that you are not running around like a chicken with your head cut off when your garage sale starts
5. What about selling coffee and donuts at your sale? Everybody loves coffee and donuts, and a lot of people don't bother getting breakfast before they leave.

GARAGE SALE SIGNS AND STICKERS

Garage sale signs and yard sale signs are vital to your bottom line. Sign design and placement are two of the most important concerns. Often, your signs alone will bring people into your sale.

Make sure that people driving by your signs can read the most important information. If you are a garage sale shopper, you know how annoying it is to try to read the information on tiny garage sale signs with small print from a moving vehicle. Do you turn your car around or back up to re-read those signs? No. You just keep on going and look for the next sale.

How do you avoid that same fate when placing your own signs?

SIGN SIZE AND DESIGN

Make your yard sale signs legible! I cannot state this any more clearly. You MUST be able to read the writing on the signs from a moving car from at least 30-50 yards away, or else your signs are worthless. Do you think the average person can read thin ink writing on a standard piece of notebook paper from a moving car? Heck no. So why do so many yard sale hosts make their signs like that?

Your sign should be at least 12 x 18", and you should make them larger, if possible. Just be careful making them TOO large, as oversized signs can be easily folded over by the wind. Some municipalities and areas limit the size of signs - I have seen 2 x 2', or 4' square. Check your cities laws before making your signs.

The print on the sign is also important. The lettering on the sign should be in legible BLOCK LETTERING, and should be BLACK, not multi-colored. Black writing is the easiest to read. You should use the largest marker that you can find, or flat black paint. The background should be a light color, so that the black writing contrasts.

Put only the information that is necessary to get people to your sale on your signs, no distracting drawings or writing. Anything that takes people's eyes away from how to get to your sale is unnecessary. Balloons and streamers are also extraneous.

Garage sale signs must relay ONLY THREE IMPORTANT DETAILS:

1. Your Street Address

2. Time and days that you sale is Open
3. What kind of sale is it?

Make sure that your days and time are large enough to be read from a distance. Do not make 'garage sale' huge and the rest of the information tiny. You also want to make sure that your letters are not mushed together, making them difficult to read. Don't use dates, so that you can reuse your signs in future years.

SIGN CONSTRUCTION

If you're willing to buy pre-constructed yard sale signs, there are definite benefits, provided you buy the largest signs, as explained previously. Professional-looking signs send several messages to prospective garage salers.

- You care about your sale.
- You are likely to have quality items to buy, because you have the money to buy quality signs

If you do buy signs, make sure that they are made of thick stock, and that the posts or frames are sturdy enough to not get destroyed by a rainstorm and can be re-used for future sales.

If you decide to make your own signs, make sure that you use materials that are weather-resistant. Paper gets destroyed by rain, almost instantly. Cardboard is a bit better, but still melts in the rain. Poster-Board is fairly reliable, but may get folded by the wind. Corrugated plastic is the best option, but can get expensive if you place the correct number of signs. I usually use poster board, and use wood posts on both sides of the signs. Make sure the bottoms are tapered so that you can drive them into the ground easily.

If you use single sided poster board, only write on one side to prevent the bleed-through effect.

Where you put your garage sale signs is almost as important as what your signs look like. The more signs that you have out, the more customers you will pull in. At a minimum, you should have signs at the nearest high-traffic intersections. You should have several signs at each intersection, so that drivers can see your signs from each direction.

If your signs are more than a mile from your road, make sure you keep drivers on the route by making small signs with arrows and your address. Make doubly sure that there is a very visible sign at the last corner before your house, so that customers do not miss your road.

GARAGE SALE STICKERS

One of my pet peeves is yard sale hosts who are too lazy to put price tags on their used items. I hate it. I usually turn around and walk right back to my car, and I know that I am not the only one who feels that way. Unless you have a large box of similar items like books or CDs, each individual item should have a large price sticker on it. The price should be clearly marked on the side of the item that is visible to the shopper. The more obvious the price sticker is, the more likely a customer is to buy it, if the price is right.

Be careful putting price stickers on collectible items like music records and posters. It's a shame to damage items by putting gaudy stickers on the collectible portions. Put price stickers somewhere that it will not damage the item when the sticker is peeled off.

There are a number of important advantages to using sharp-looking manufactured yard sale stickers, like the ones seen above left. Here are some considerations:

- The faster you can price your garage sale items, the more time you have to find more stuff to sell. Time is money! It's more than twice as fast to peel and stick manufactured price stickers than to make your own price stickers.
- Manufactured yard sale labels look better, and the better and more organized your garage sale is, the more likely it is that people will feel good about buying your stuff. Make your sale look good!
- Color coding of price stickers allows rummage sale hosts to easily keep track of multiple family's sales, sales in multiple categories (red for books, green for

music, etc.), and you could even use a certain colored sticker for items leftover from prior garage sales that you are still trying to get rid of.
- Price stickers are cheap. You really are not saving much money by using good price stickers rather than a roll of tape and an ink pen.
- Now with the ease of ordering labels online, you can order in two minutes and have labels delivered right to your house. You don't even have to go to the store to get them!
- Manufactured Garage Sale Stickers are highly visible. Customers that can see item prices easily are much more likely to pick up and buy an item that is for sale than an item that has the price sticker obscured.
- Manufactured price stickers are safer on collectible items than sticking masking tape on them, or (God forbid!) actually writing on the items with a marker. Try to avoid sticking ANY stickers on the dust jackets of books, especially antiquarian books. Stick your labels inside the book on the blank interior page, or better yet, use a chart like the one in the photo above and to the right to avoid putting stickers on books. You also want to avoid putting stickers on vinyl record jackets, collectible posters, and anything else that is antique and made of paper or cardboard. Think of your customers who are collectors when you are pricing your items!

GARAGE SALE PRICING

Garage sale pricing is the most vital factor in determining profits, and how much clutter you will get rid of! The challenge in yard sale pricing is to make the most money possible, while not frustrating customers pricing garage sale items higher than what they are used to seeing at typical garage sales and yard sales.

The fact that you are taking the time to read this e-book shows that you are in the upper 10% of garage sale hosts. You are making the extra effort to do some research into improving your yard sale. I can't tell you how many sales that I have been to where it is obvious that the host has put no thought or effort into their sale. Half of their items are not priced. There are full boxes lying all over the place. Half of the time, I can't even tell what is for sale, and what is not. Don't be one of these people!

It's important to adjust your garage sales prices to reflect the condition of your items. Make sure that mechanical items work, and items have all of their pieces. Don't offer items for full price, if they are worn. Don't try to make an extra dollar at the expense of your customer, if you know the item is not fully functional. Price those items to move. Make your money on collectibles, media items, and good quality kids and women's clothes. I will tell you that if I get to a sale and I see a bunch of overpriced items, I usually leave. I don't waste time haggling. It is an excellent idea to visit a number of garage sales to see what other hosts are using for garage sale prices on commonly sold items, so you know the ball-park that you should be starting in for your own garage sale pricing. We have also provided a fairly large list of commonly sold items and their average prices sold for at garage and yard sales in our Garage Sale Price Guide.

GARAGE SALE PRICING GUIDE

This Garage Sale **Pricing Guide** is a garage sale and yard sale price list of many commonly sold garage sales items. The prices shown are average prices from around the country, for items that are in average used condition. If you live in an upscale neighborhood, you may wish to raise prices 20% from the values provided.

A general rule of thumb is to reduce your price by 20-30% from the buy price listed on the garage sale pricing guide for each year that you own consumer electronics like TVs, computers, video game systems, etc. You should also take at least 50% off of the listed price for items that have major flaws like missing pieces, chipped glass, cracked plastic, missing power cords, missing CD and video game cases, etc.

These prices listed in the garage sale pricing guide are determined by going to thousands of garage sales, and buying these used items for reselling on eBay or for personal use. This is a sampling of items, to give you an idea of where to start for your garage sale pricing or yard sale pricing.

Media Items

Hardcover Books - $1-2 - Check all pre-1950 books, coffee table books, and newer texts on Amazon

Softcover Books - .25 or 5 for $1 Check all newer texts on Amazon.

Audio Books / CD Books - $1

Music CDs: - $1, unless rare. Sell in Bulk lots.

Vinyl Records: .25 - .50 for commons, $1+ for Rock, Blues, and Cult Soundtracks - Check records before selling. 45 RPMS generally less

Cassette Tapes / 8 Tracks: .25-.50 - Better to list in bulk for $5-10. Limited demand.

CD Storage Racks, Spinners: $3-10+ These sell for $20-50 on Amazon for large 100CD units!

DVDs - $1 for older to $5 for newer titles

Clothes

Kids Clothes - $1, $3-5 for Name Brands

Baby Clothes - $1-3

Women's Tops - $1-5

Men's Tops - $1-3

Name Brand Jeans - $5-10

Other Jeans - $1-3

Sweaters - $3-5

T-Shirts - .50 - $1

Tennis Shoes - $1-5, more for newer Nikes, etc.

Dress Shoes - $1-3

Women Shoes - $1-20, vary greatly by maker

Jackets, Outerwear - $3-10

Suits - $10 for outdated, to $50 for newer

Snow Boots - $1 for older, to $10 for good newer.

Household Items

Kitchen Appliances - $3-10

Dishes - Sets $10, individual 0.25-.50

Tupperware - 0.25 - $1 for large

Flatware - Sell in lots $1-3

Serving Dishes - $1

Good Pots, Pans 0.50 -$1

Wall Decor, Framed Art - $1-5, small. $5-10 Lg

Large Appliances - $25-50 (Fridges, ovens, etc. that work

Microwaves - $5-20

Picture Frames, Mirrors - 0.25 - $1

General Household - $1

Collectibles

Avon, Homco, small Knick-Knacks: $1

Collectibles Plates $.50 - $1

Pottery - $1-5

Longaberger Baskets - $3-10, more for older

Swarovski Crystals - $5-20 for large

Beer / Food Collectibles - $1-5

Collectible Prints - $5-10

Sports Cards - Check eBay

Sports Memorabilia - Check eBay

Entertainment Memorabilia - Check eBay

Video Games & Systems

Newer Video Games (PS3, Xbox 360, Wii, Dreamcast) - Check Amazon for prices, they vary greatly. Popular titles at least $10-20.

Video Games 5+ Years Old (PS2, Xbox 1, Game Cube, Super

NES, Etc. - $1-3

Outdated Video Games (PS1, Sega Genesis, Nintendo 64) - .50 -$2, Classic games $5

Classic Video Games (Nintendo NES, Atari 2600, 400, 800, Colecovision, Intellivision) - $2-4, check all of these games, some are worth over $100!

Video Game Systems: Always sell for more on eBay or Amazon. Do not sell these at garage sales, unless you need immediate money.

Minimum for systems with no games: PS3, Xbox 360 $100, Wii $60, Classics $40-50, Outdated $20-30, 5+ $30-40. Newer handheld $40-60, older $20.

Newer Controllers: $5-15 (PS3 are $40 new)

Older Controllers: $1-2

Power Cords, AV cords, Remotes, etc.: $1

Toys and Games

Board Games - 0.50 - $2, more for electronic, and some newer high-end games.

Legos, Building Sets - These can bring big $$ on the internet. $5 for small lots, up to $20 for large

Handheld Electronic Games - $.25-$1

Barbie Dolls - Older can be highly collectible. Newer $1-3, clothes, accessories $.25-$5 for vehicles.

Stuffed Animals, Dolls - $.25-$1 for high-end

Action Figures - .25 -$1, Transformers $1 small, up to $10 for large new figures

Hot Wheels, Matchbox Vehicles: Some are highly collectible. Newer - Sell in lots 10/$1

Vintage Toys - $1-5

General Toys - .25

Holiday / Christmas

Ornaments - .25-$1, Hallmark Keepsakes in box $1-5 for collectibles like Star Wars, Wizard of Oz, etc.

Vintage Ornaments - $.50-$2

Artificial Xmas Trees - $10-40

Lights - .25-$1.00, depends on length

General Xmas Decor - $.50 - $2

Halloween Costumes - $1-10 for newer popular

Outdoors

Power Tools - $5-20 for working with batteries

Power Tool Batteries, Chargers - $2-5 for newer

Lawn Mowers (Push) - $10-20

Lawn Mowers (Riding) - $30 minimum

Bikes - $5-10 for kids, average. Check eBay for high-end bike prices

Sports Equipment -$1-5

Fishing Poles - $1 Cheap to $10 for name brand and large Salt Water, Salmon Rods

Fishing Tackle - $5-20 for full boxes

Small Landscaping, Garden Tools -$.50-$2

Long Handled Tools- (Rakes, Shovels, etc.) - $2-5

Small Tools -(Screwdrivers, Hammers, etc.) 0.50 -$1

Pet Supplies - 0.50 - $2

AFTER YOUR GARAGE SALE: GETTING RID OF YOUR STUFF FOR FREE

After your garage sale is over, what do you do with all of the unsold items? There are still ways for you to make money on your unsold items!

Well, I'll tell what you do NOT want to do! Do NOT pack the stuff back up and put it back into your house, storage shed or barn. You want to GET RID OF THE STUFF. That is why you have a garage sale in the first place. So... how do we accomplish the task, and maybe make a little bit of money on your leftover stuff?

Here are some options for garage sale, yard sale, rummage sale, and estate sale hosts for garage sale cleanup:

1. DO NOT PAY MONEY FOR GARAGE SALE CLEAN-UP. There are many ways to avoid this. There are many people advertising on Craigslist that will pick up your leftover stuff for free. You can also set boxes at the road with a FREE sign. Somebody will pick up the boxes.
2. Re-Check everything you have left after the garage sale for items that you can sell online (or somebody else you know can sell it, if you don't want to). Most media items can be sold online on eBay or Amazon.
3. Keep stuff together by category. If you have boxes full of books, music, holiday decor, name brand clothing, etc., make a quick listing on Craigslist, and tell people you have a large lot of whatever you have for $5. Somebody will buy it.
4. You can take boxes of books to Used Book stores and get something for them. Take boxes of CDs or records to used music shops.

5. Another excellent idea is to coordinate with another future garage sale hosts. Is your neighbor going to have a large garage sale in a couple of weeks? When is your local community or church sale? See if you can drop off your good leftover items for their sale! You may have to help with set-up or something, but it is worth it.
6. Most cities have a Boy Scout or other organizational benefit at some point in the summer. You can drop off boxes of stuff for them to sell and claim a donation on your income taxes. See below.
7. BEFORE YOU THROW STUFF IN THE TRASH, YOU CAN WRITE OFF USED ITEMS DONATED TO CHARITY FOR EXCELLENT INCOME TAX WRITE-OFFS. Check **Itsdeductible.com** for a large list of IRS-approved, acceptable donation amounts for commonly donated items. You will be very surprised at how much you can write off! It's is definitely worth the time it takes to register on the site, and make your list of items for donation. Make sure that you take digital photos of the boxes and items for your tax records.

YARD SALE TIPS

Here are some yard sale tips to help you make the most money at your sale this year!

1. When you hold a garage sale, you are primarily protected inside of your garage. Yard sale hosts have to account for the weather. Make sure that you have a Rain Date in your advertisements, usually the following weekend.
2. Make sure that you keep boxes somewhere that you can get them out fast, in case it rains. You will want to have all of your items out of the boxes and priced before your sale starts, but lay out items so that you can easily put them back into a box in a hurry.
3. Get some waterproof tarps lined up before your sale. The bigger the tarps, the better. You can also use the tarps to cover your items after each day, so you don't get rain, dew, or dust on your items.
4. You have a lot more flexibility in how you organize tables, compared to a garage sale. Make sure that you give people room to pass each other comfortably in between the tables. You should set up your tables so that there is a flow to your sale, and shoppers end up naturally at your pay table.
5. I've been to a ton of sales that look like a bomb went off in the hosts' yard. Make your sale look neat, and people will feel more comfortable buying stuff from you.
6. Assign one host to be the organizer. She can keep your items looking good, which will directly need to more sales! Keep moving items to the fronts of the tables as stuff sells. You don't want large open spaces on your tables. Eventually, you will want to remove tables

when they start looking thin. The organizer can also make sure that price stickers are visible, toys are not where people can trip on them, and even perhaps make a run for drinks and food!

7. Chances are, you and your potential customers are going to be in the hot sun. Schedule your sale when it is not going to be 100 degrees. June is better than August in the US.
8. You can make some quick money by selling coffee when it is cool, or lemonade when it is hot. Better yet, have the kids do it!
9. I like having the toys table or area at the front of the sale, and off to the side. That way, your customers' kids are quickly satisfied, and they will often grab toys at the front of your sale just to shut the kids up, so they can shop. It also contains the mess off to the side, and keeps the rowdy kids from your book shoppers, who are often older adults.
10. For summer sales, start early. You will have early birds there before 7AM anyway, so start at 7. It is likely to be cool in the morning, and many people like to get things done in the summer while it is still tolerable. Research has shown that sales often slow considerably after noon. I like the 7-3 time slot for summer sales.

CONCLUSION

The proceeds from this document are dedicated to our children's college funds. I greatly appreciate your interest in my product. Please recommend this book to your friends and family. If you have a couple of minutes, please take the time to leave me five star feedback on Amazon for this document by going to your account, and leaving a feedback / review for the order. Make sure that you continue and read the last couple of pages, which contain some excellent links to websites that you should visit for even more tips. Good luck in your future endeavors, Eric Michael.

I would like to invite you to brag about your treasures found and partake in discussions about garage sailing and re-selling at the Almost Free Money Facebook http://www.facebook.com/almostfreemoney

and Garage Sale Academy Facebook http://www.facebook.com/garagesaleacademy pages.

WEBSITES AND LINKS

Here are some very helpful websites and web pages to jump start your research. These are my favorites, after completing many hours of surfing (You are welcome!)

1. Garage Sale Academy

http://www.garagesaleacademy.com

Our website has a ton of information about how to become a garage sale picker, and how to resell your garage sale finds on the internet. It expands the information from Almost Free Money by adding an entire niche on garage sale picking / shopping, and tons of information on how to get the best deals at sale, and find the best swag. It also has another niche for increasing the productivity of garage sales, yard sales, and estate sales for sale hosts. Garage Sale Academy also has links to the rest of the books in the Almost Free Money series, a garage sale forum, and a garage sale blog.

2. Its Deductible

https://itsdeductibleonline.intuit.com

As discussed in Donations section. Provides IRS-accepted values for your donations, and keeps track of your donations for the entire tax year. Inserts your donations into online Income Tax forms such as TurboTax.

Made in the USA
San Bernardino, CA
18 July 2013